1

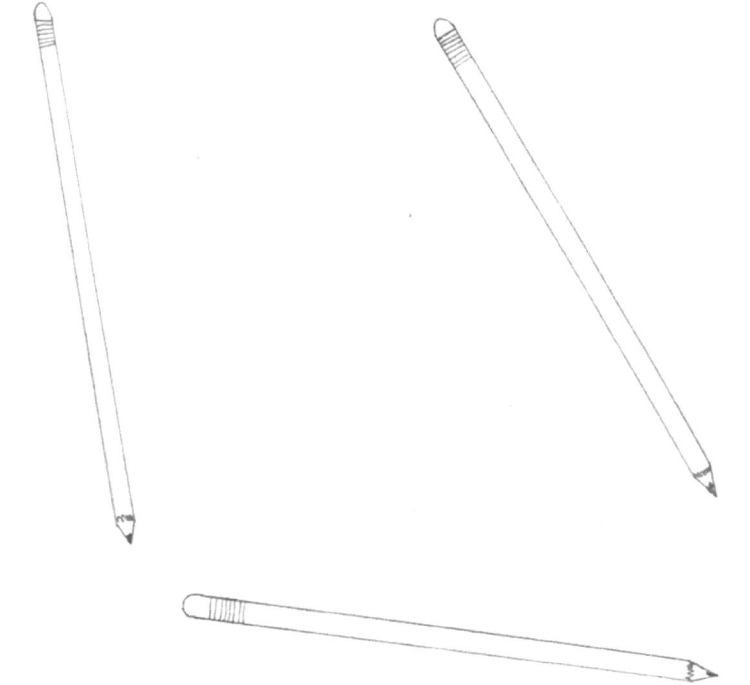

Decorative Dreams
A Drawing Collection
By Frank Temple

2/2

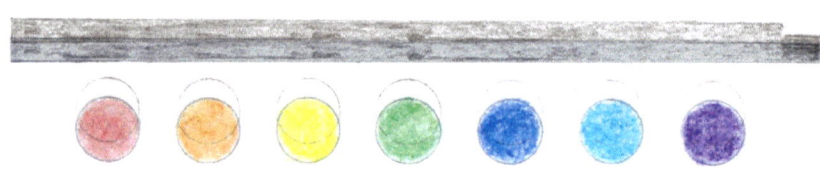

Introduction:

People respond to shapes and symbols. It is part of out human intelligence. Colors affect our emotions. It is apart of our sensitive feeling nature. Here is a collection of pencil drawings and crayon subjects to stimulate the reader's imagination. Some of these I have been drawing for many years. Instead of a book full of wordy text, I have escaped words to a degree into the realm of original creative art. As I enjoyed doing this book, I hope the readers finds it to their liking.

As a child I made drawings. I used crayons, pencils, and water colors to create images. Teachers in school taught me symbols, systems of knowledge, useful things, and cultural material. Here as a mature man I have returned to drawing again. The creative spark is behind it all.

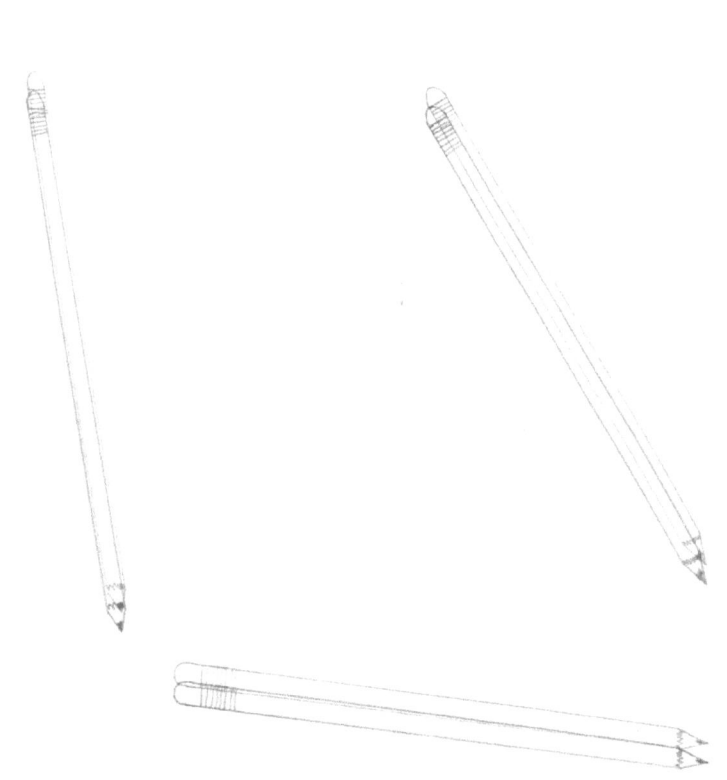

4

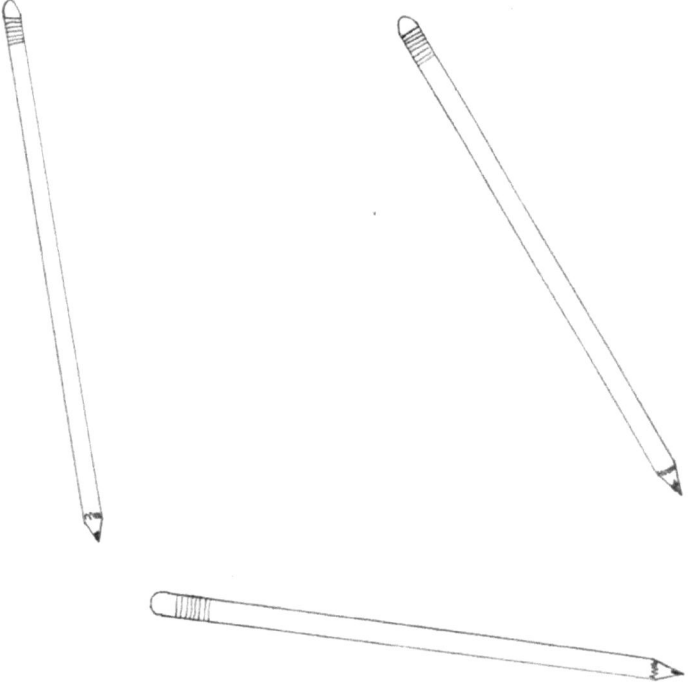

Pencil Drawings:

Art is line and color. These very talented pencils created all of the following group of drawings.

5

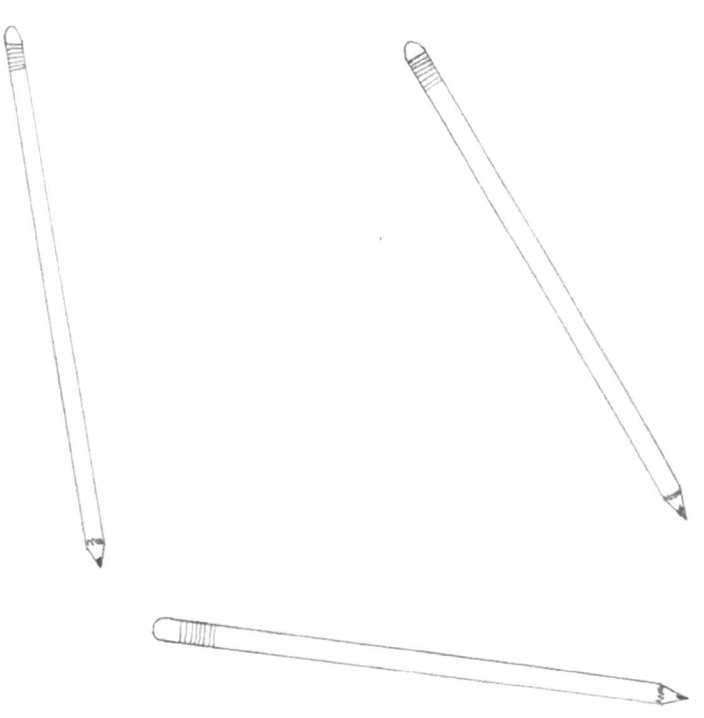

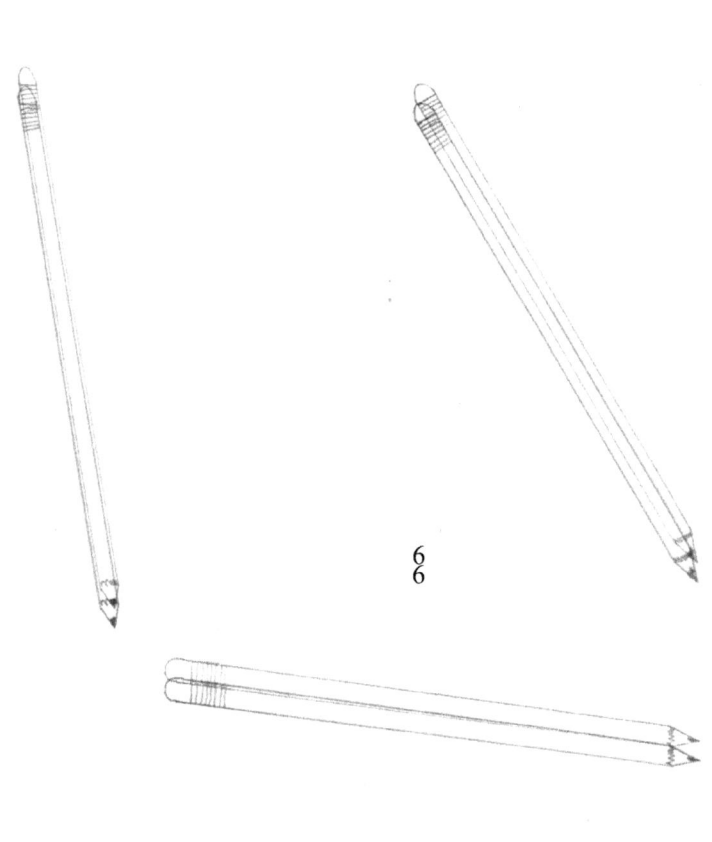

Helicopter
Helicopter

7

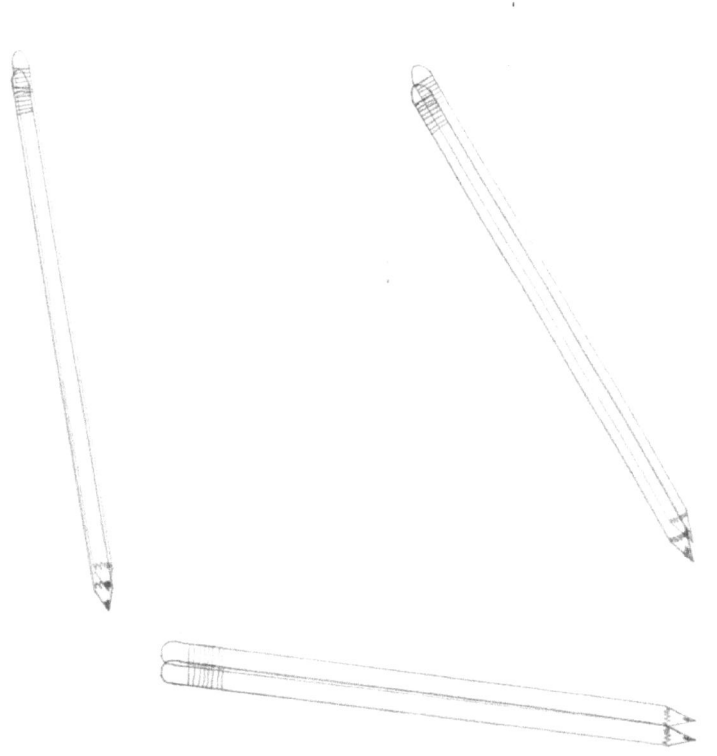

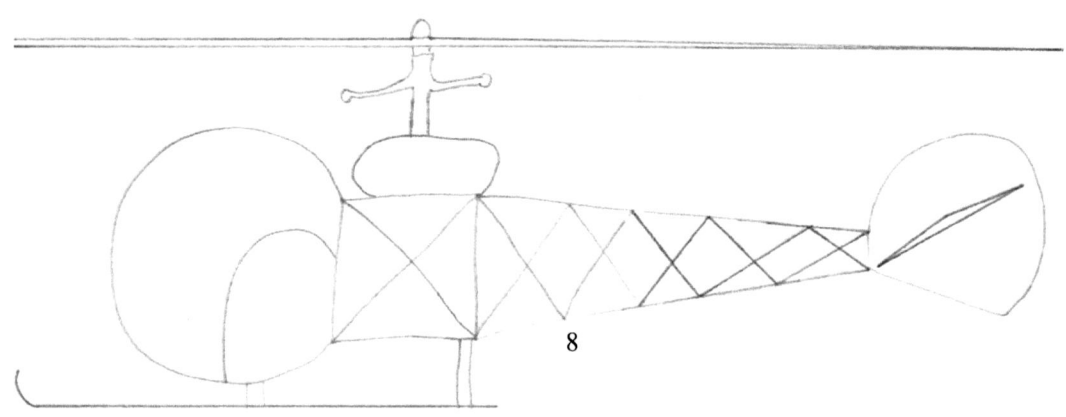

8

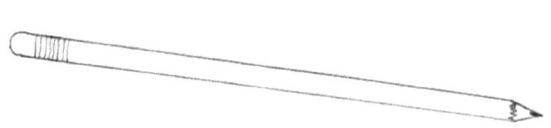

Mountains

9

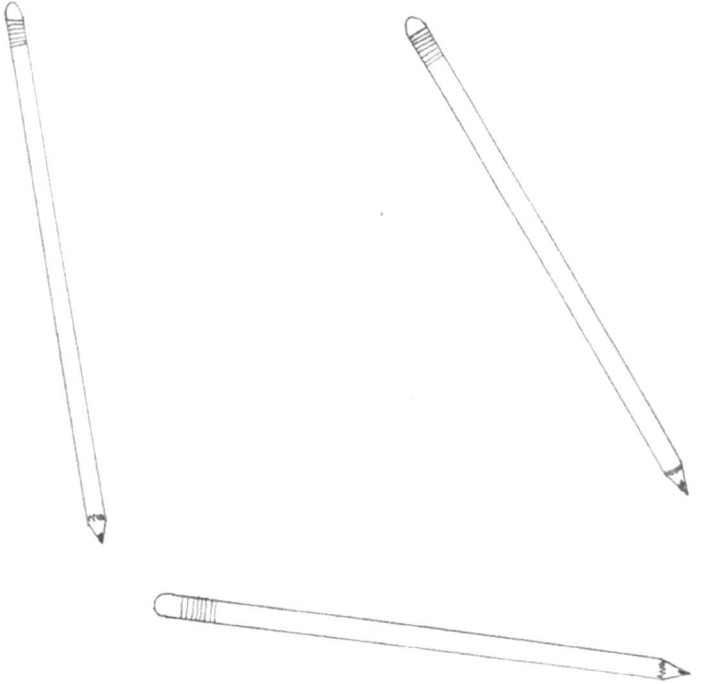

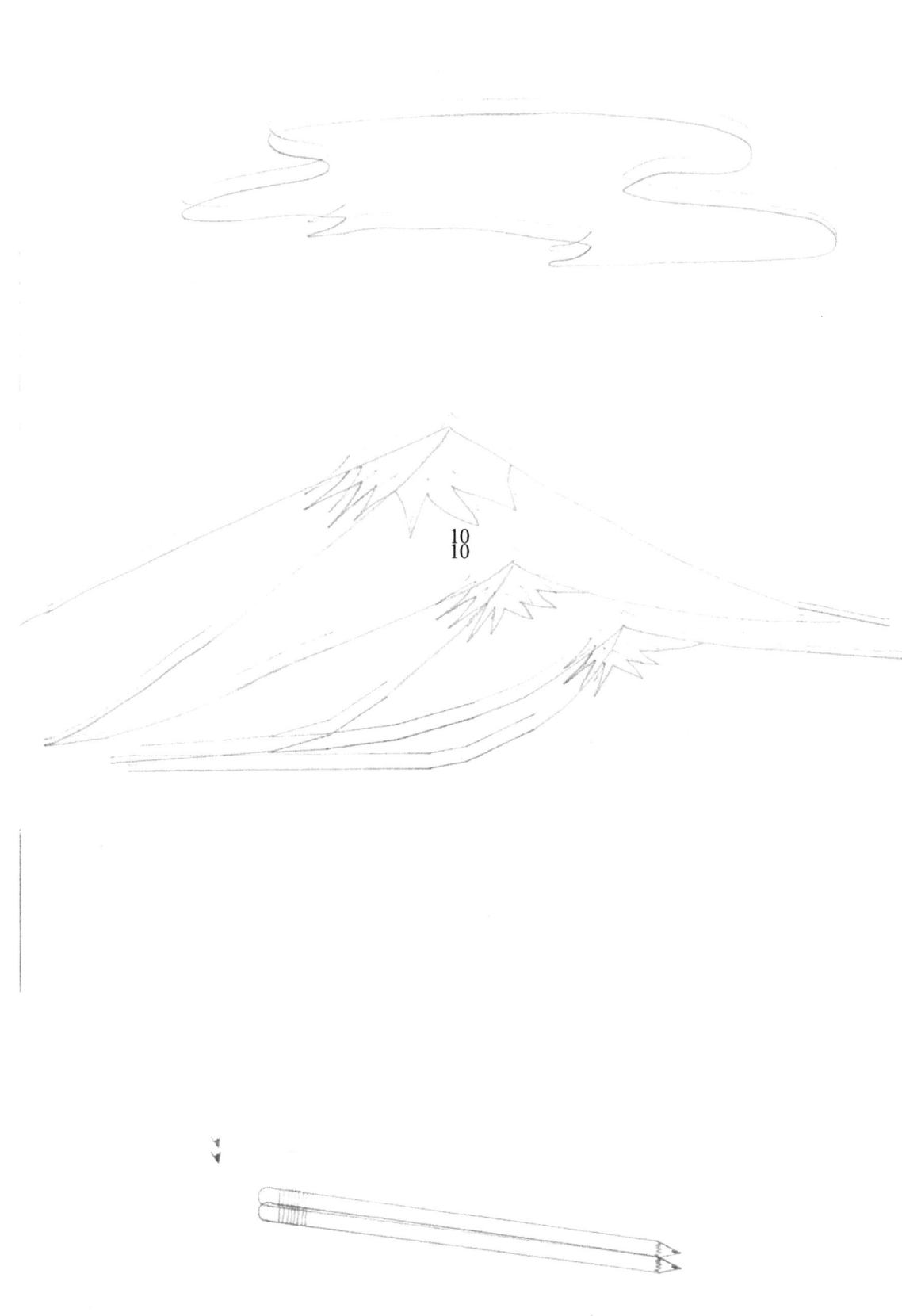

Cat
Cat

11
11

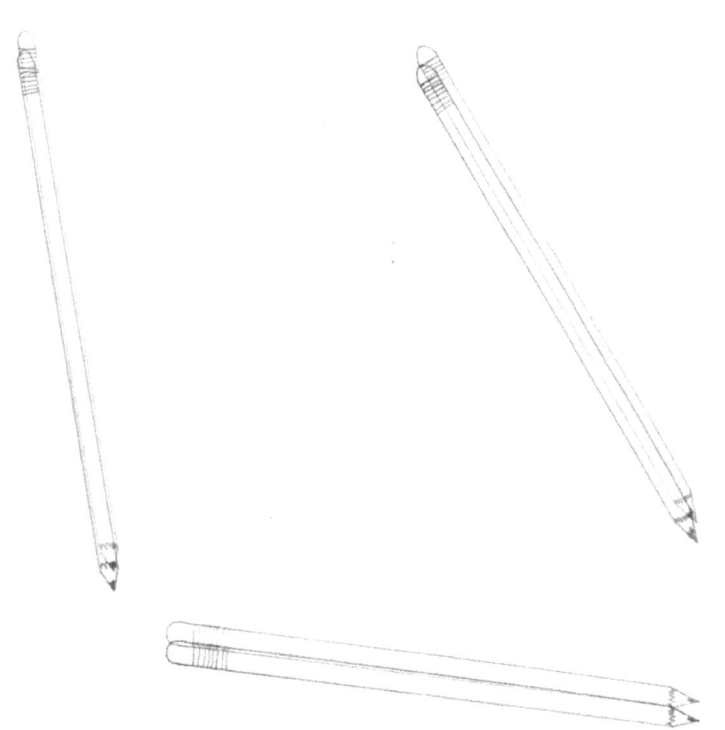

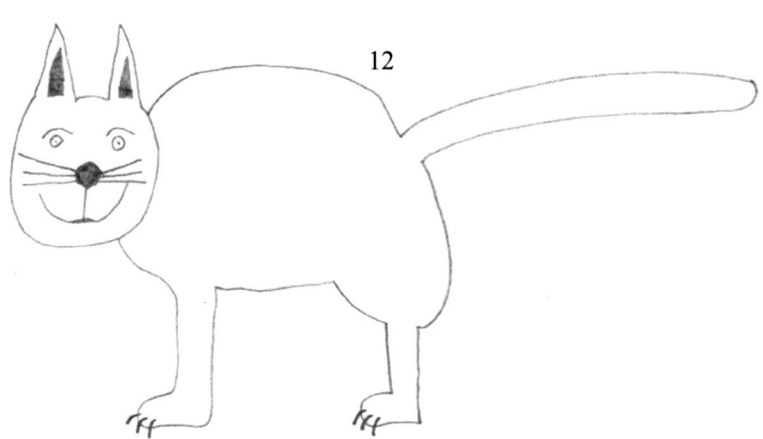

12

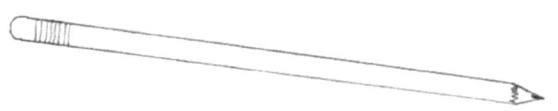

Clown

13

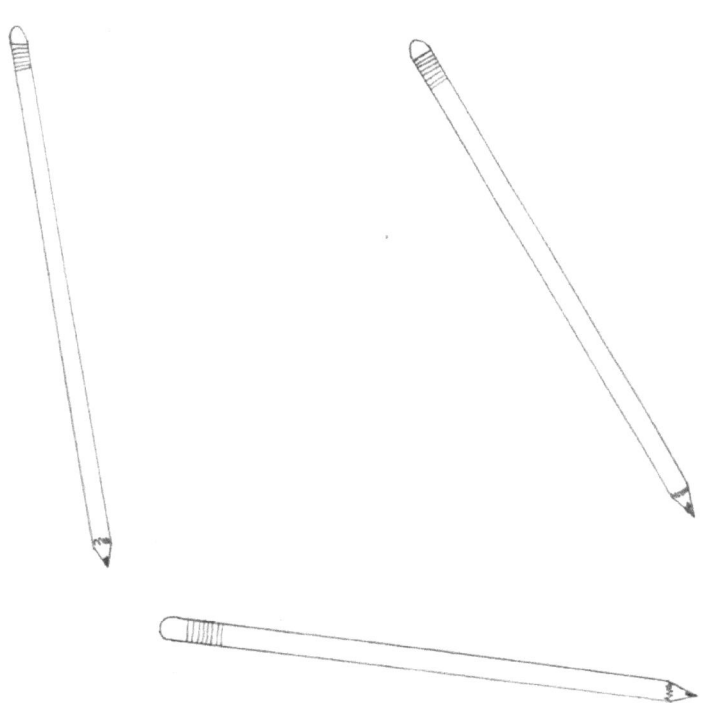

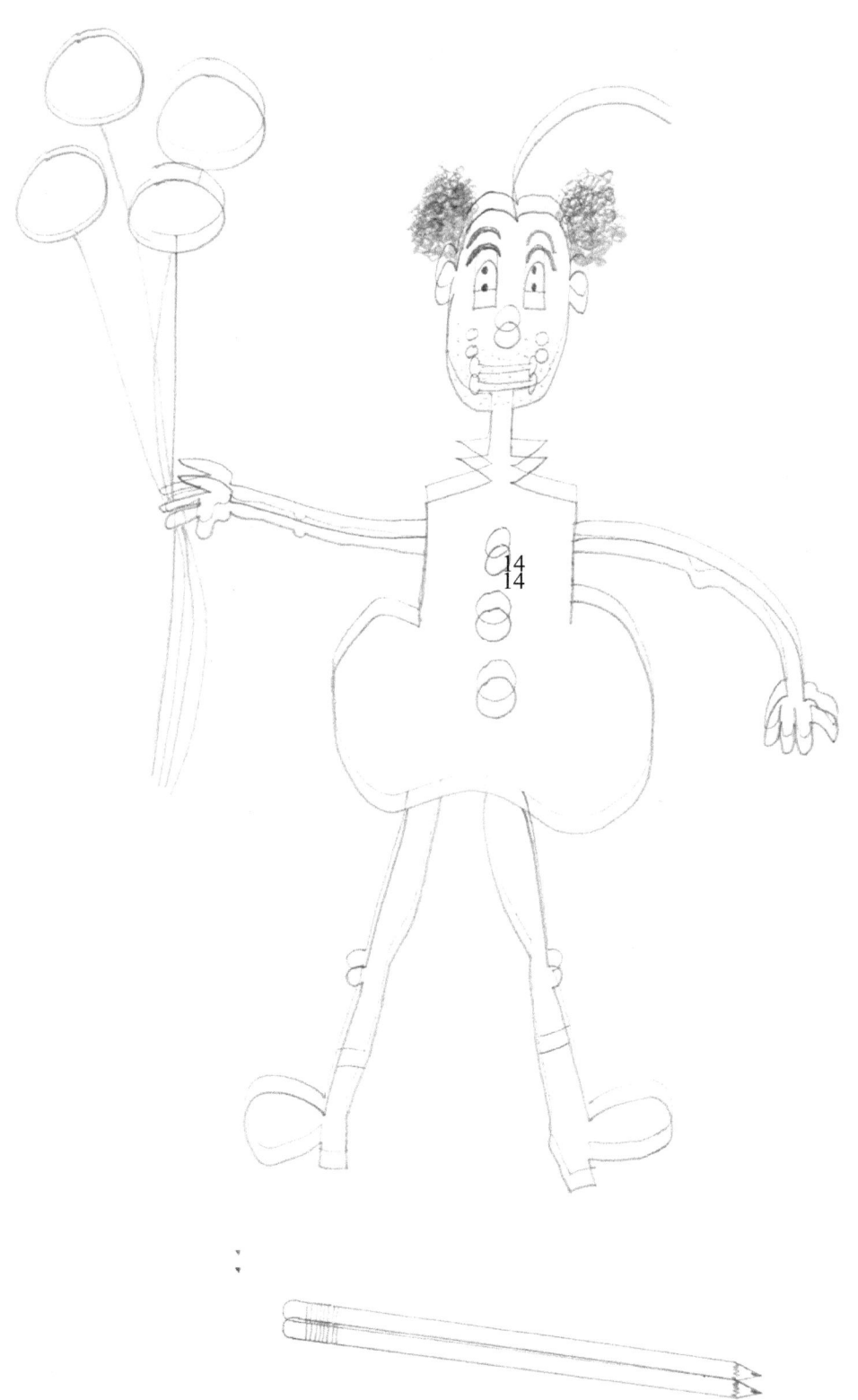

Car
Car

15
15

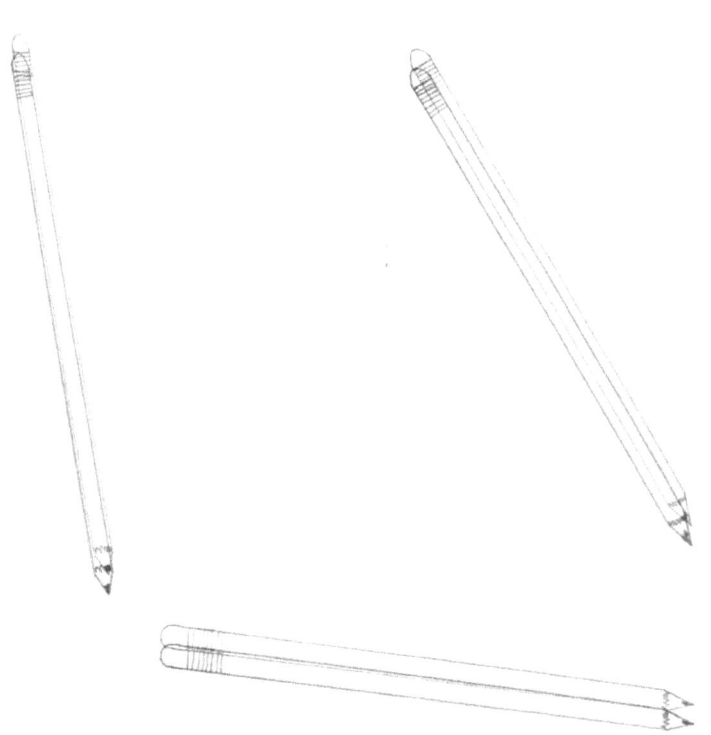

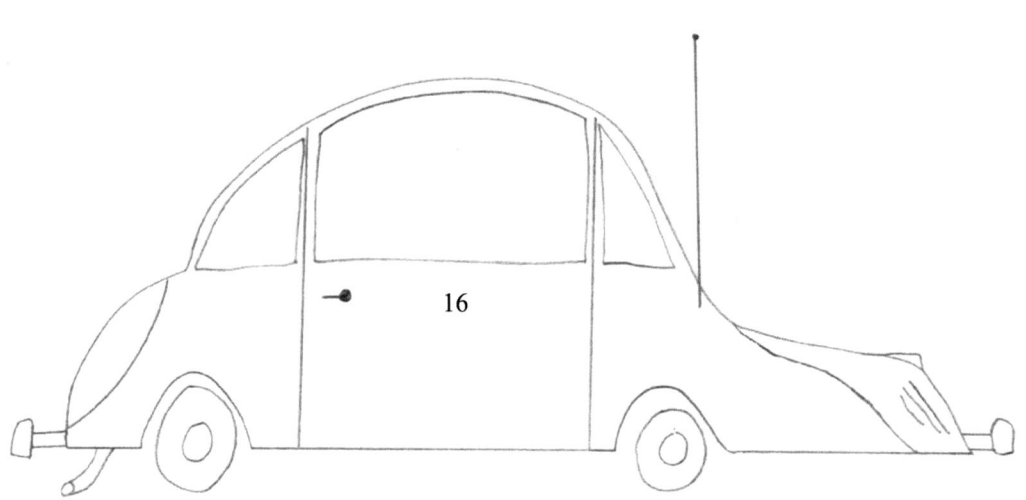

16

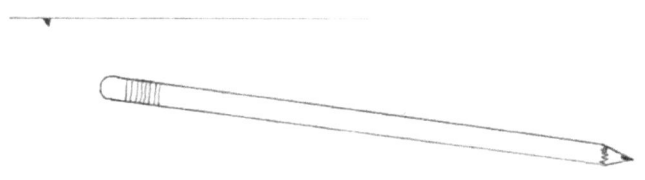

Rocket

17

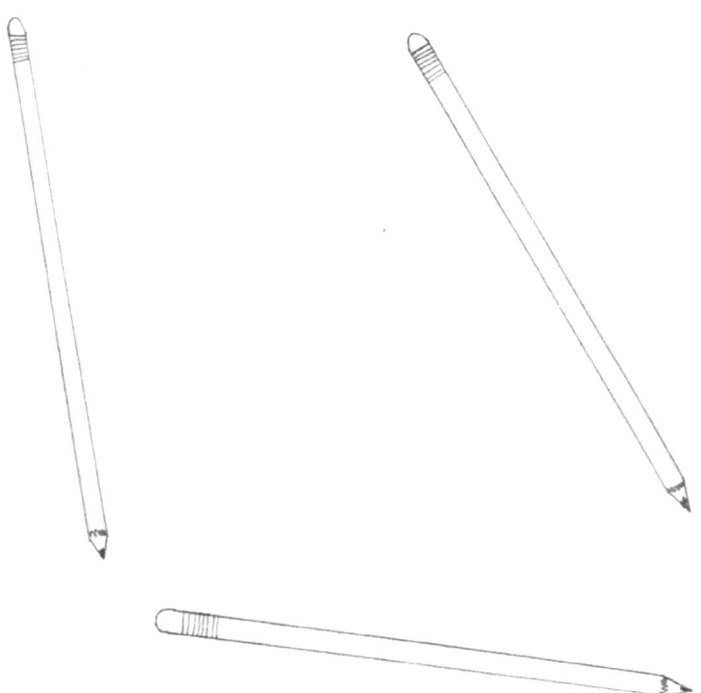

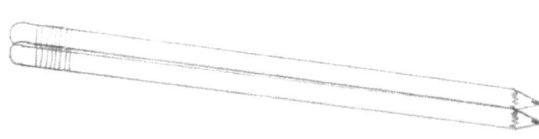

Dog
Dog

19
19

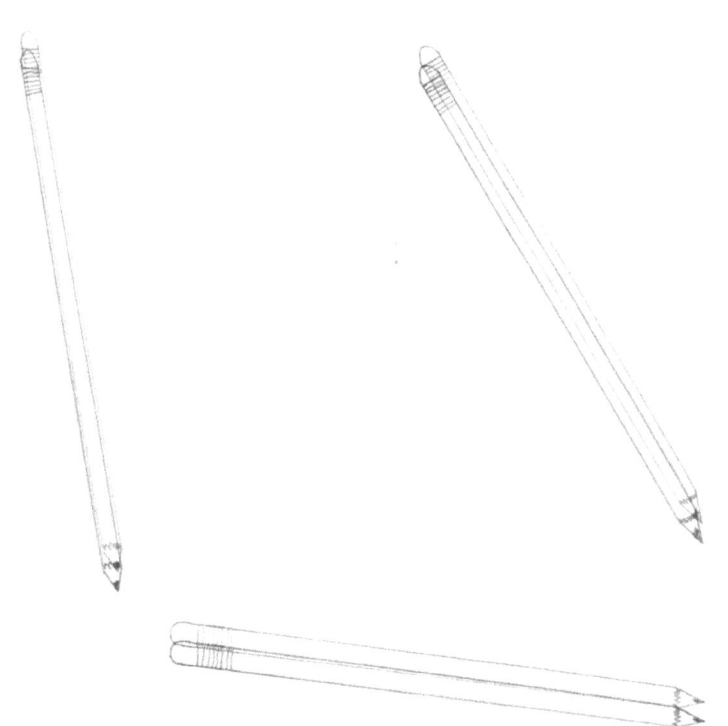

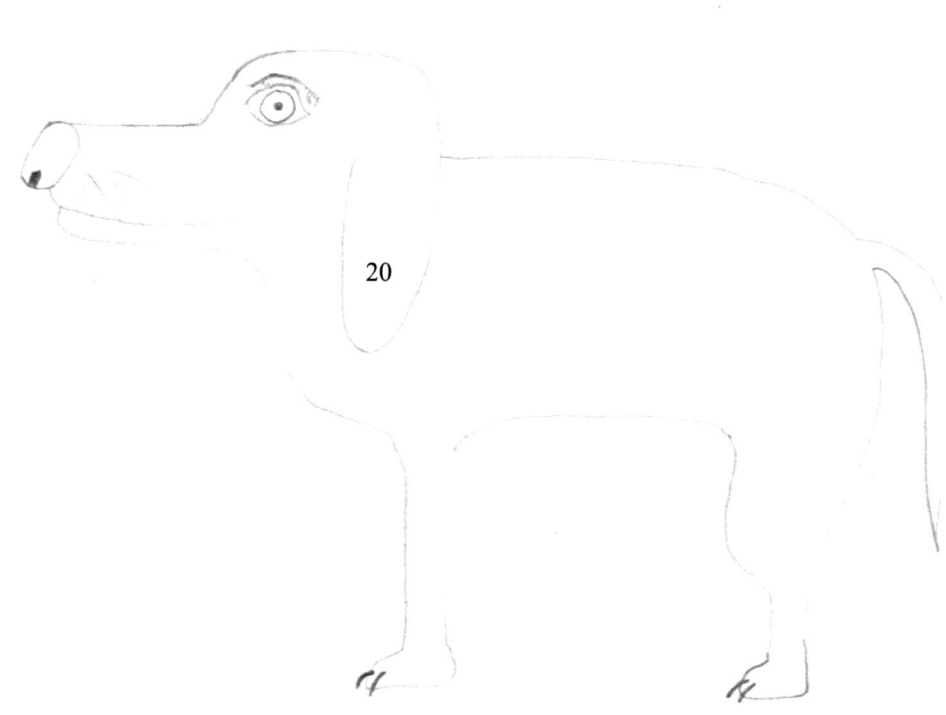

Horse

21

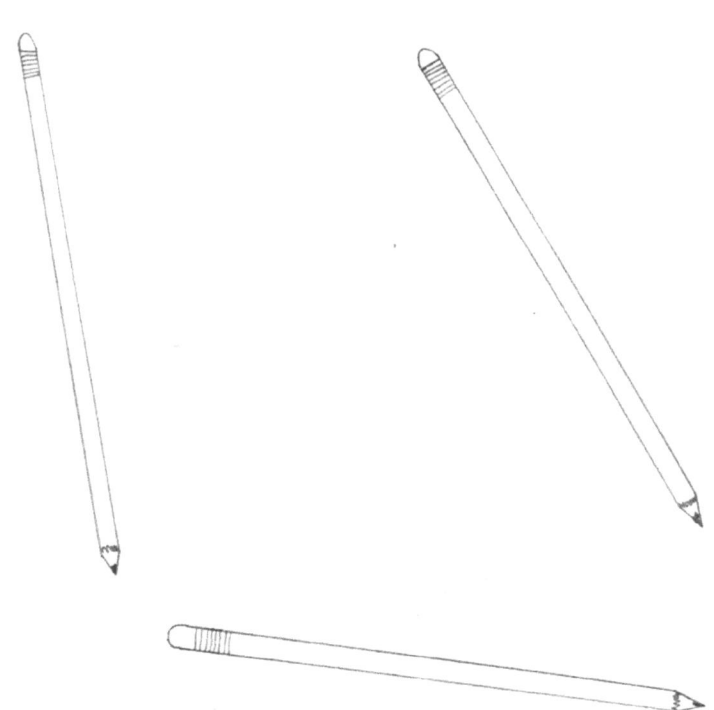

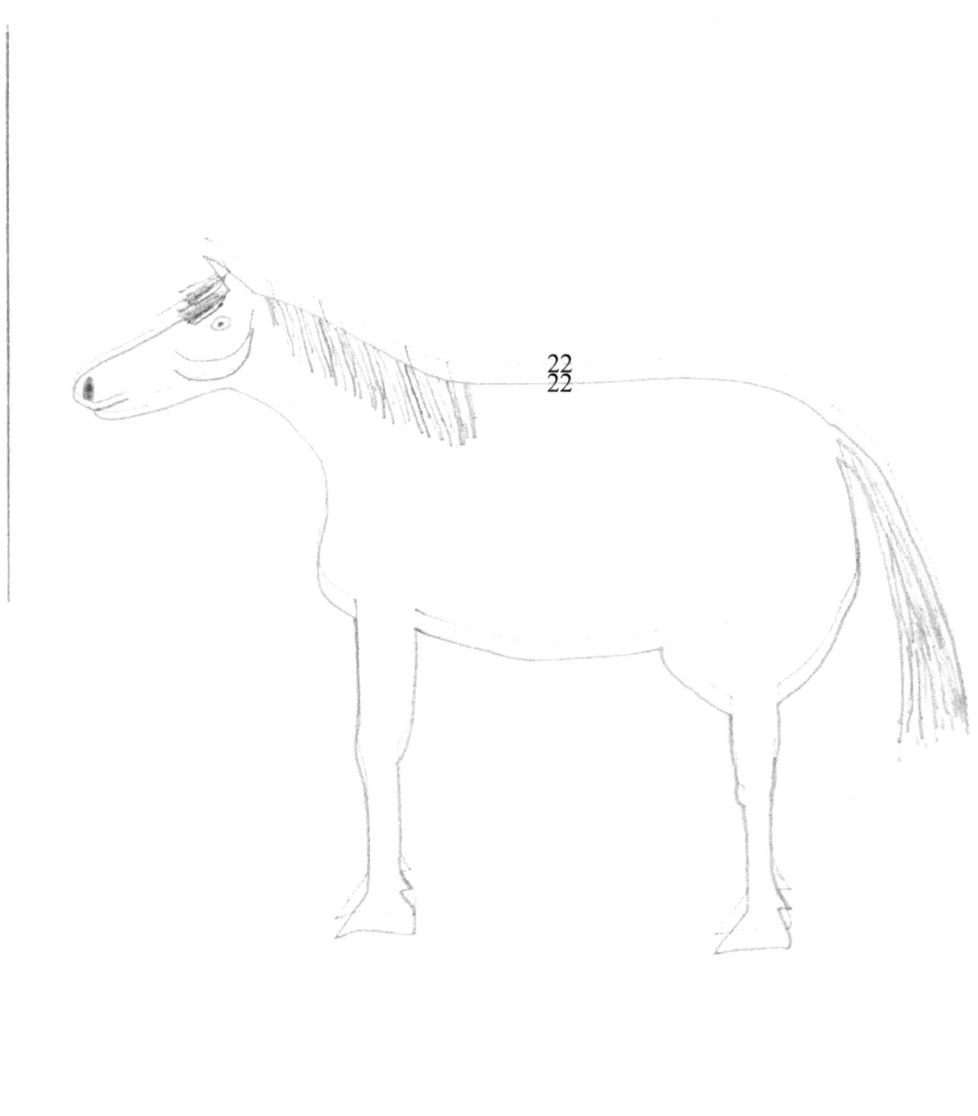

## Country Cottage With Mill Pond

23

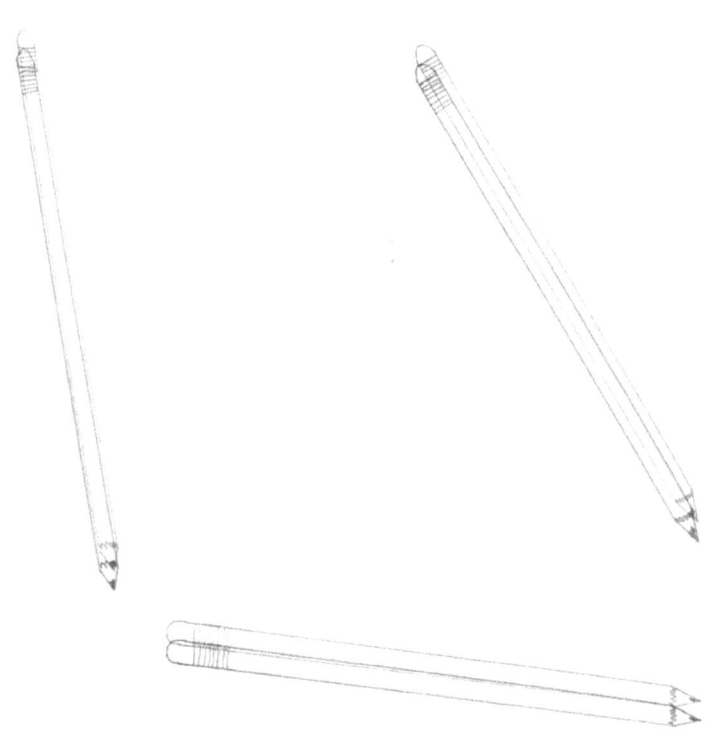

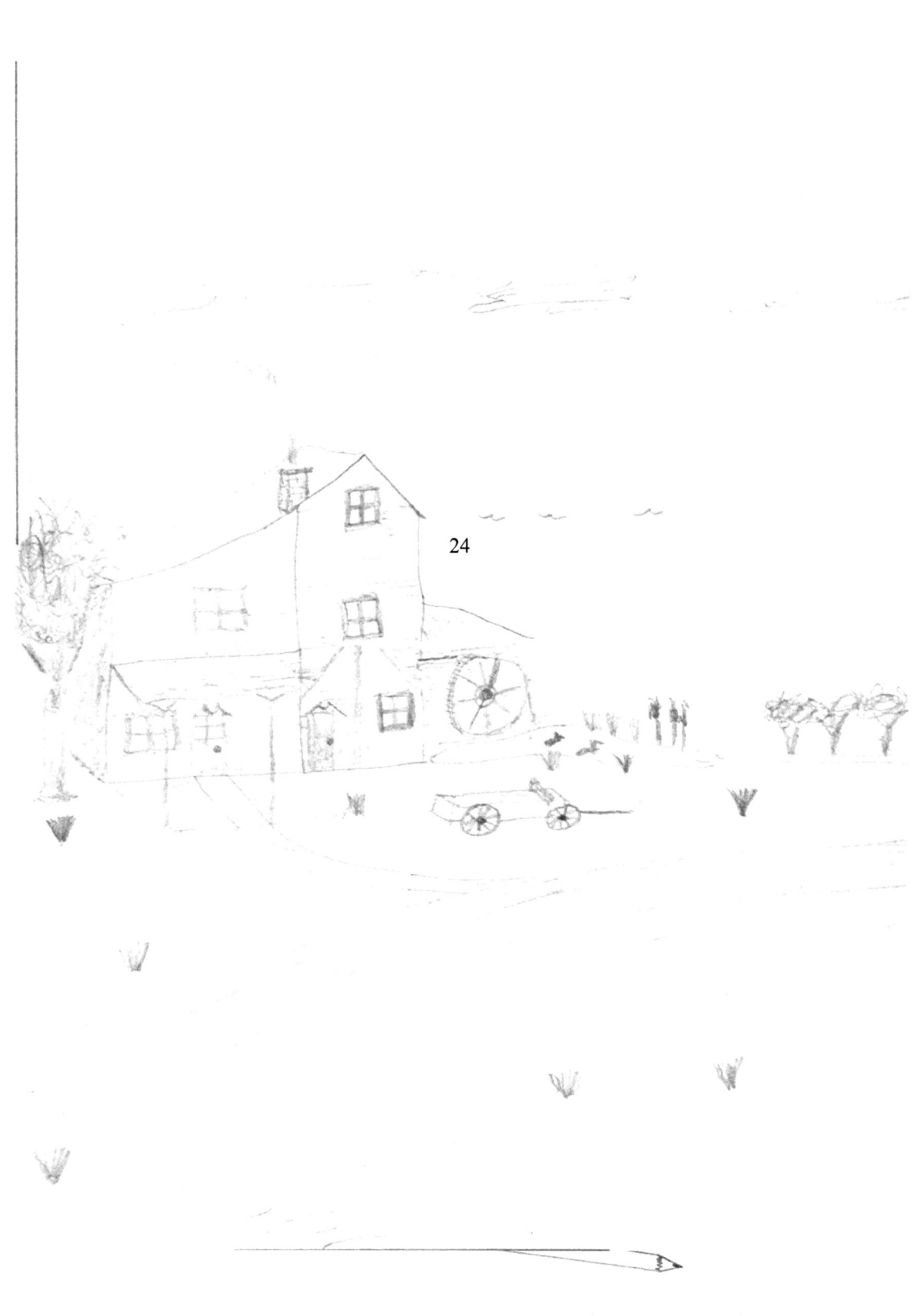
24

House

25

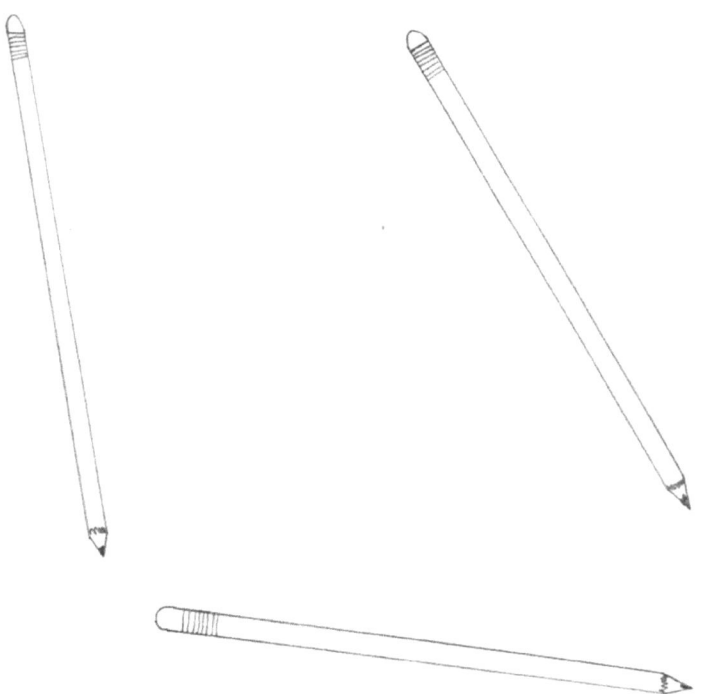

Tree
Tree

27
27

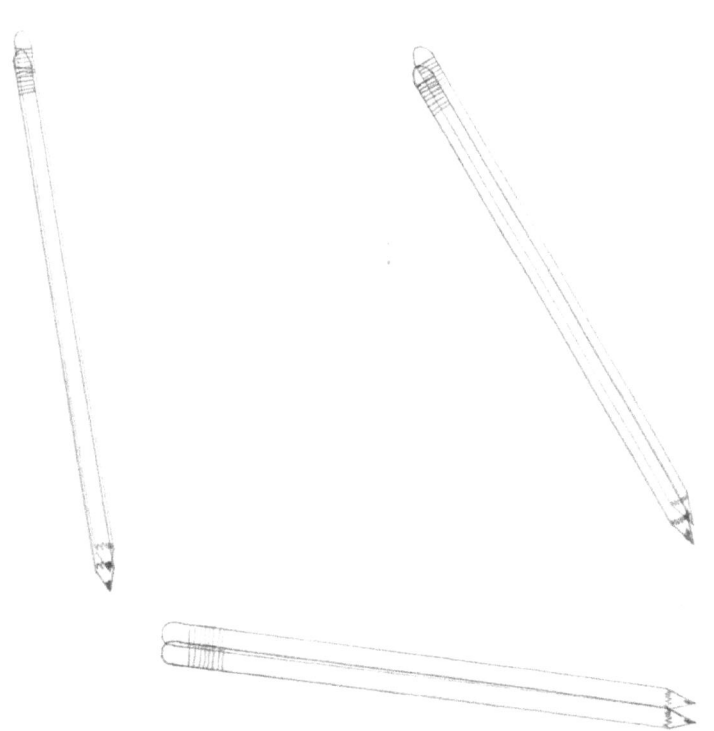

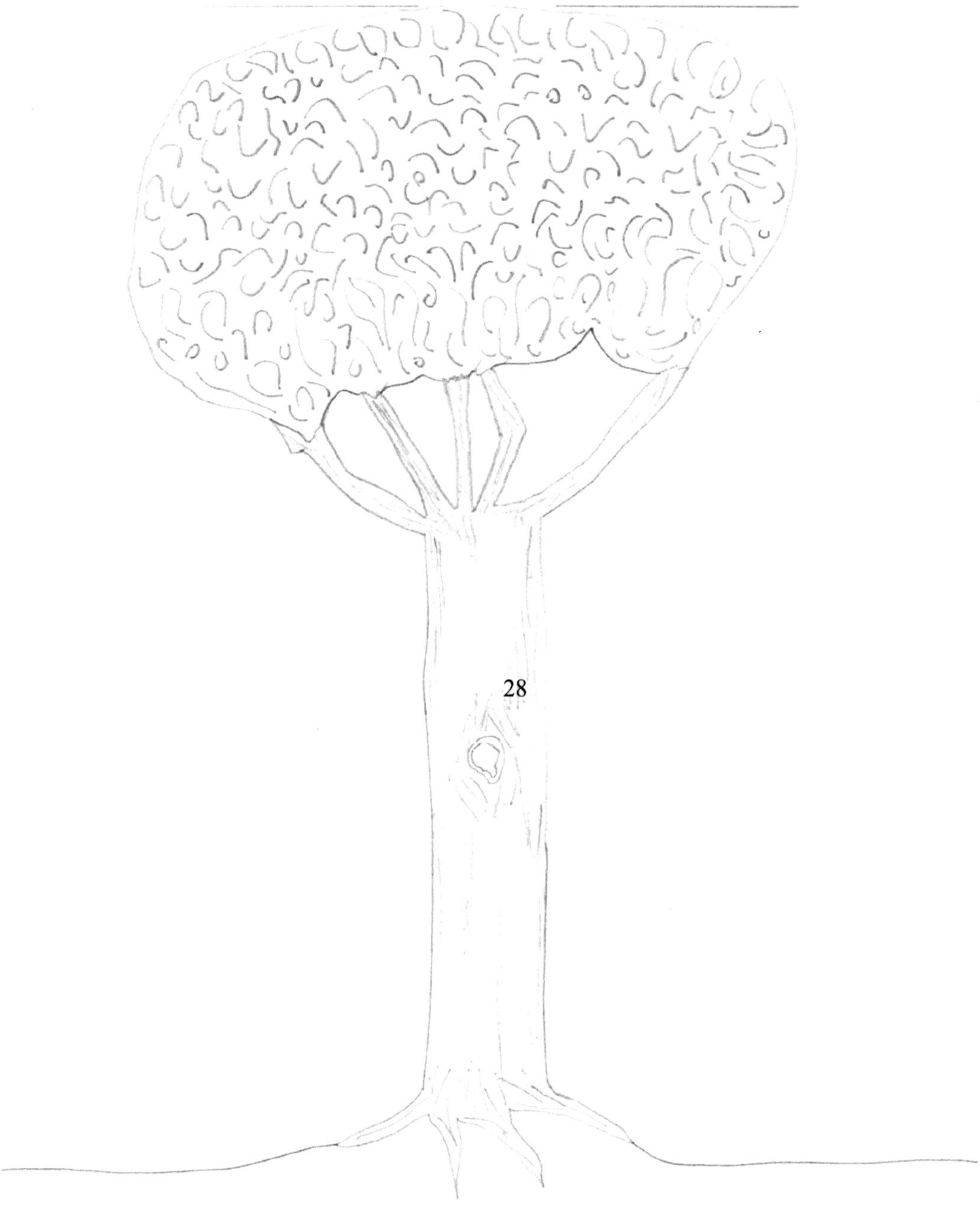

28

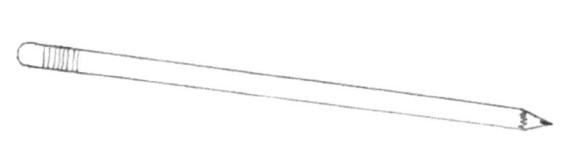

Flower

29

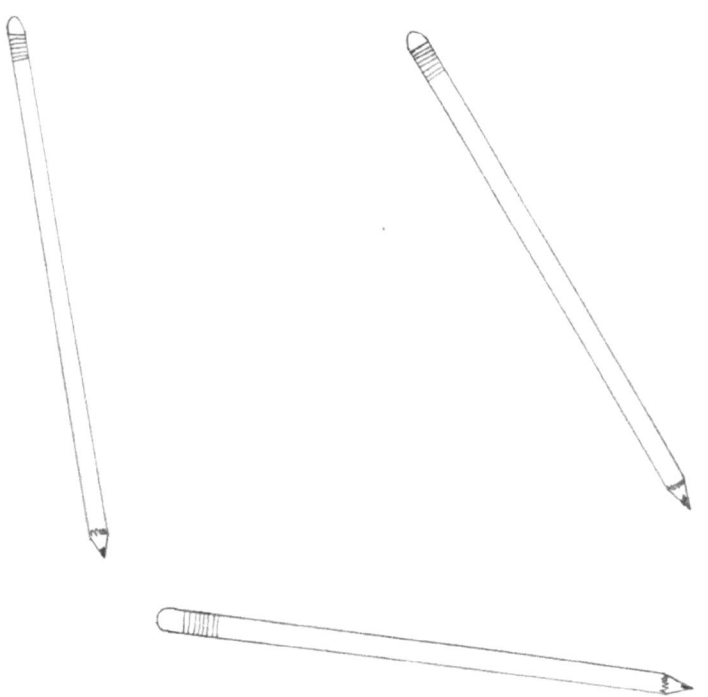

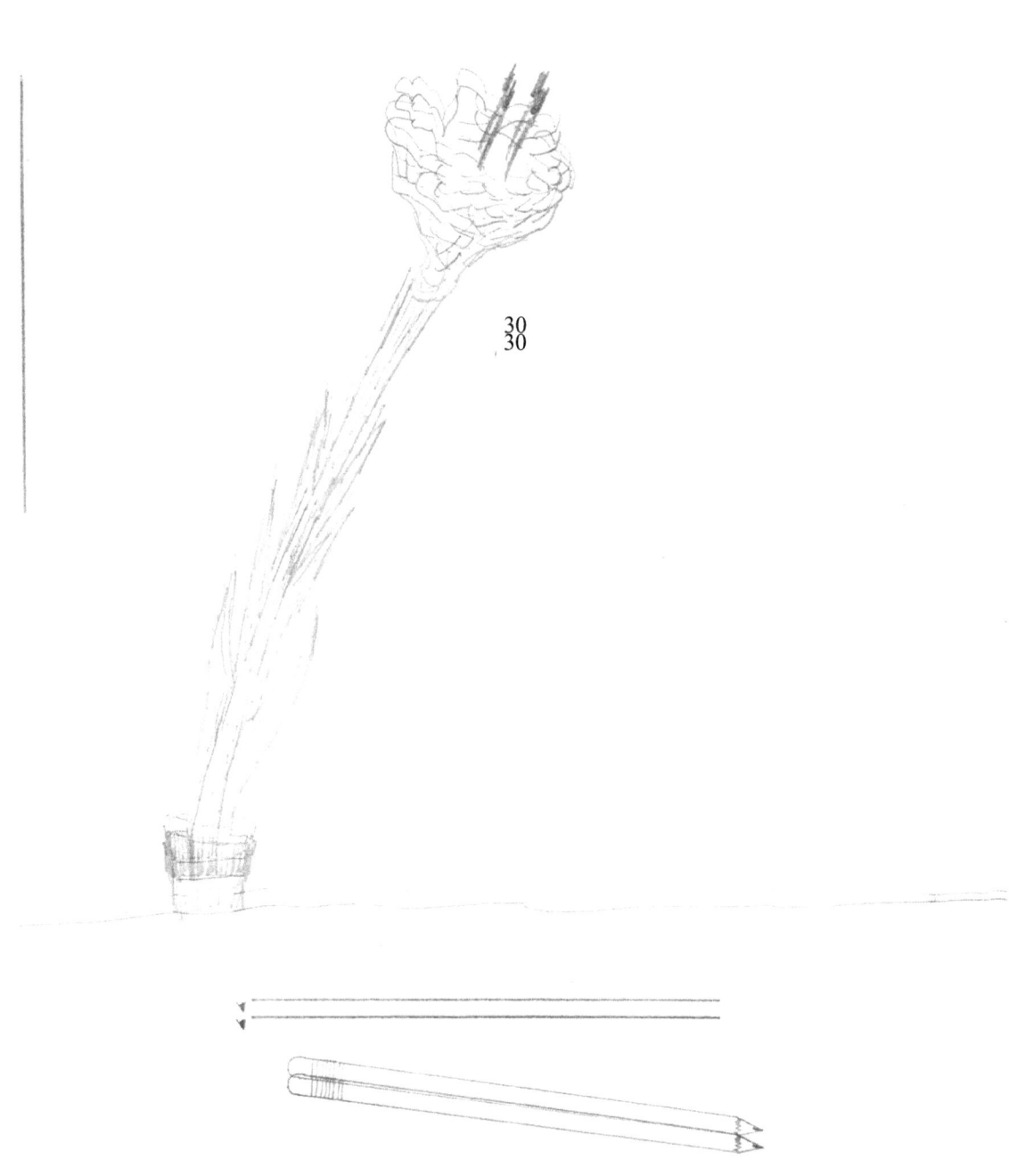

Desk And Chair
Desk And Chair

31
31

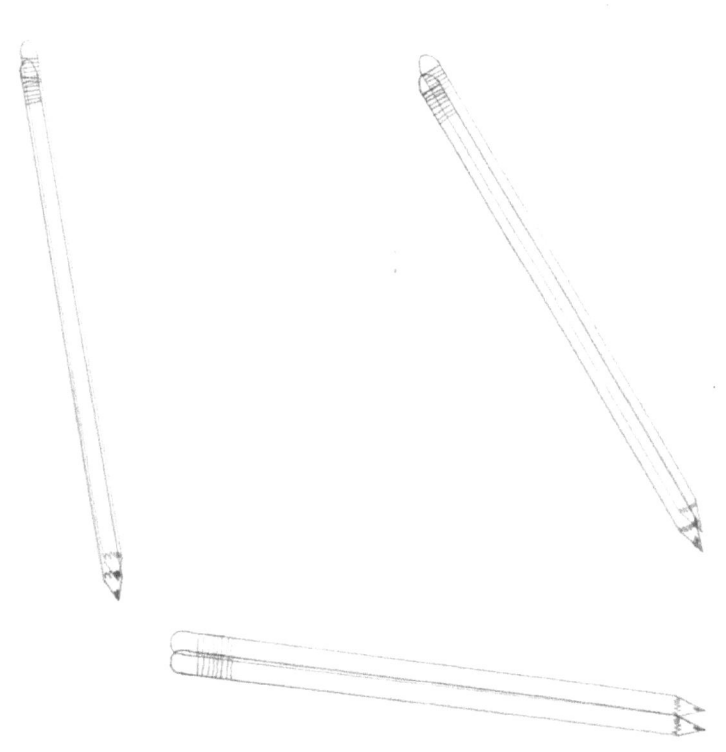

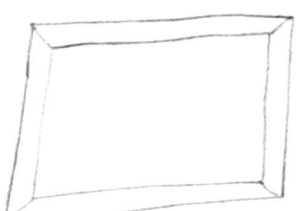

32

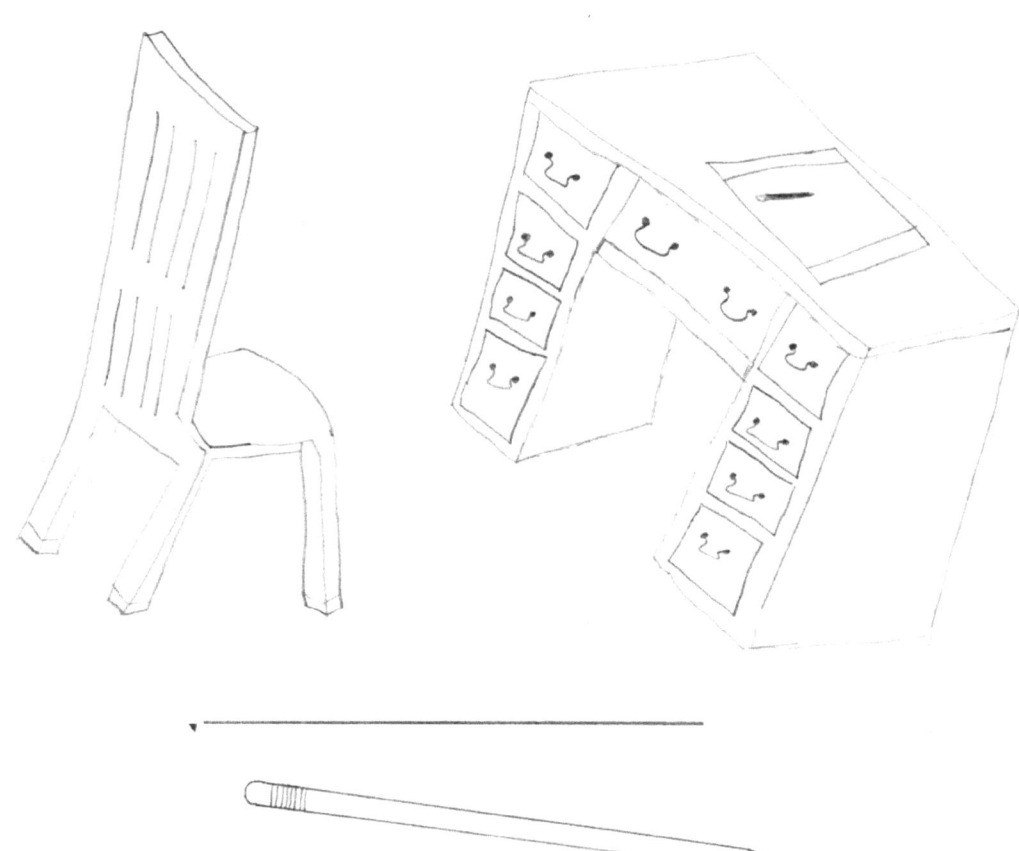

Boat

33

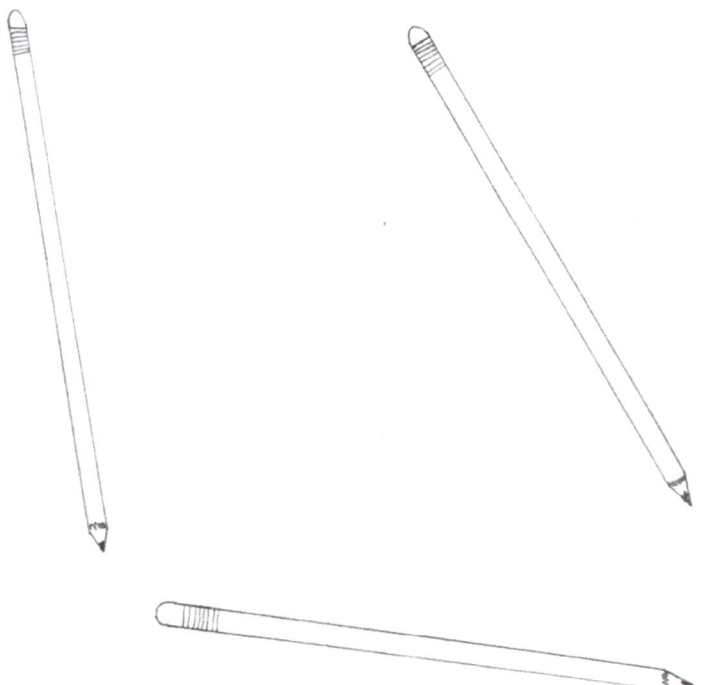

34
34

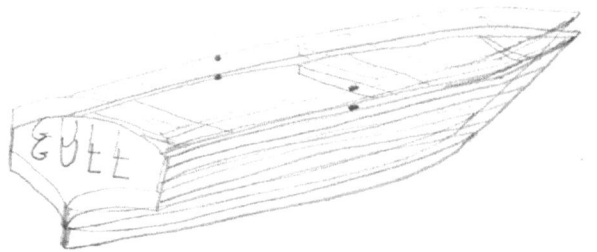

Rock Bridge
Rock Bridge

35
35

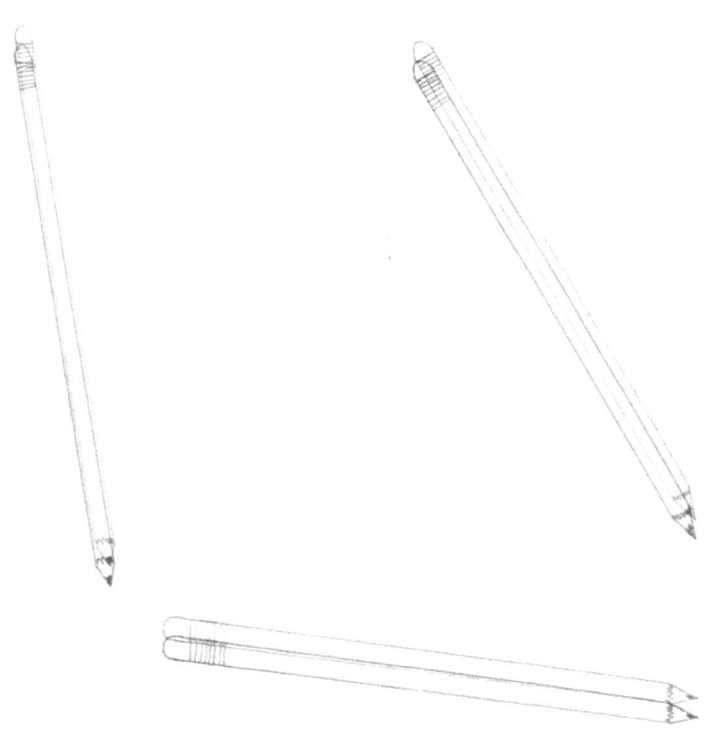

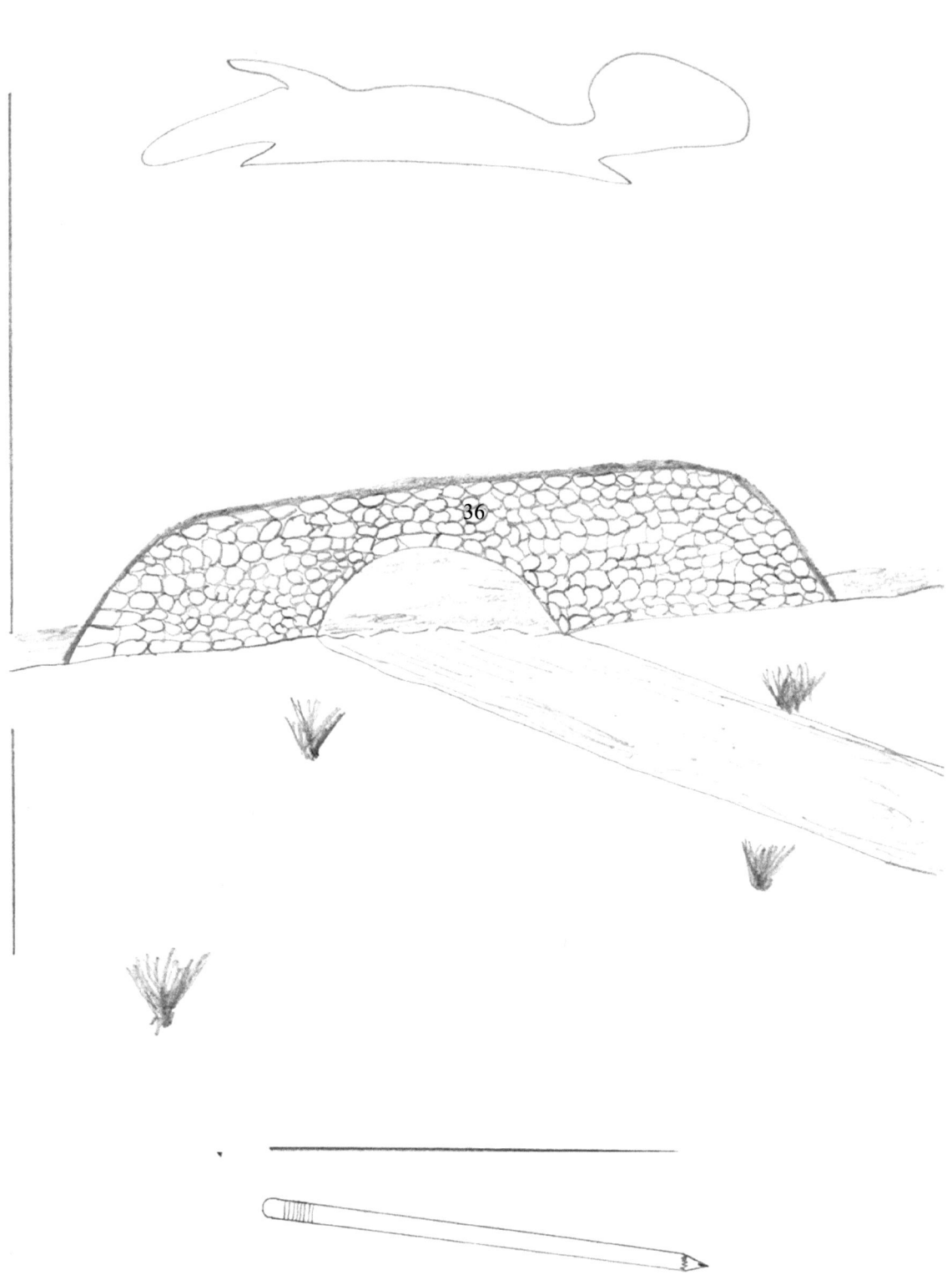

Monster

37

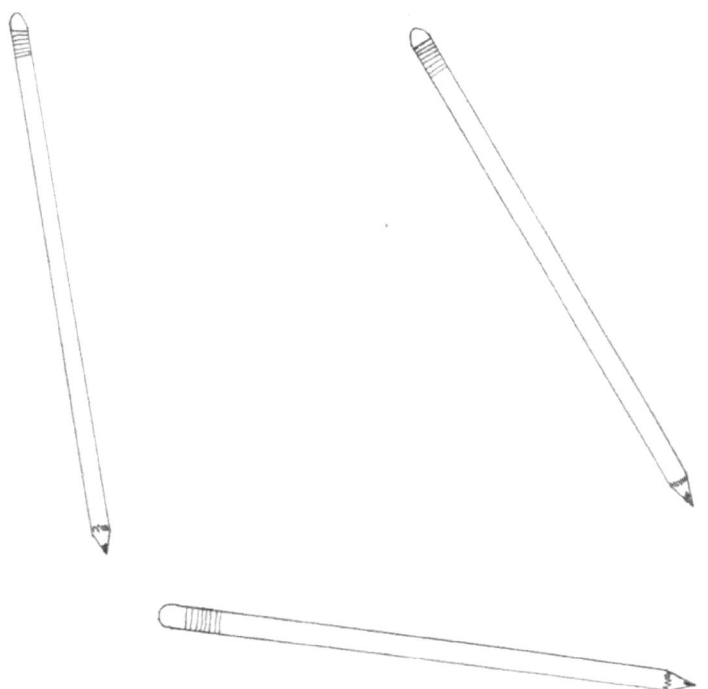

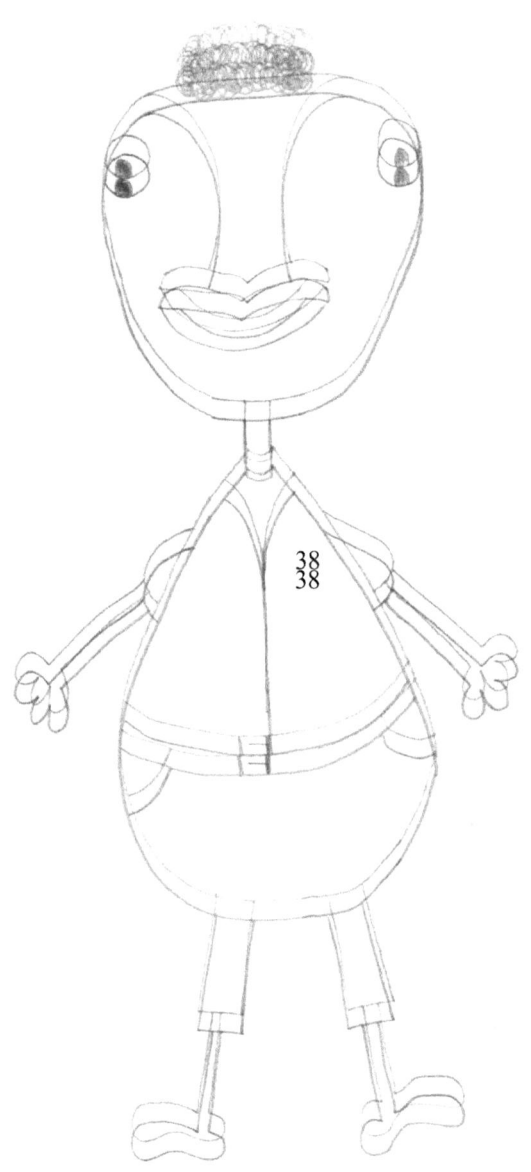
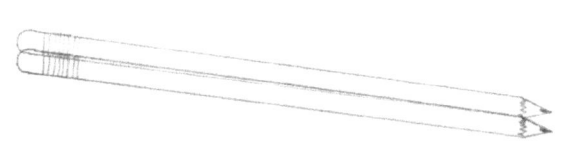

Ghost
Ghost

39
39

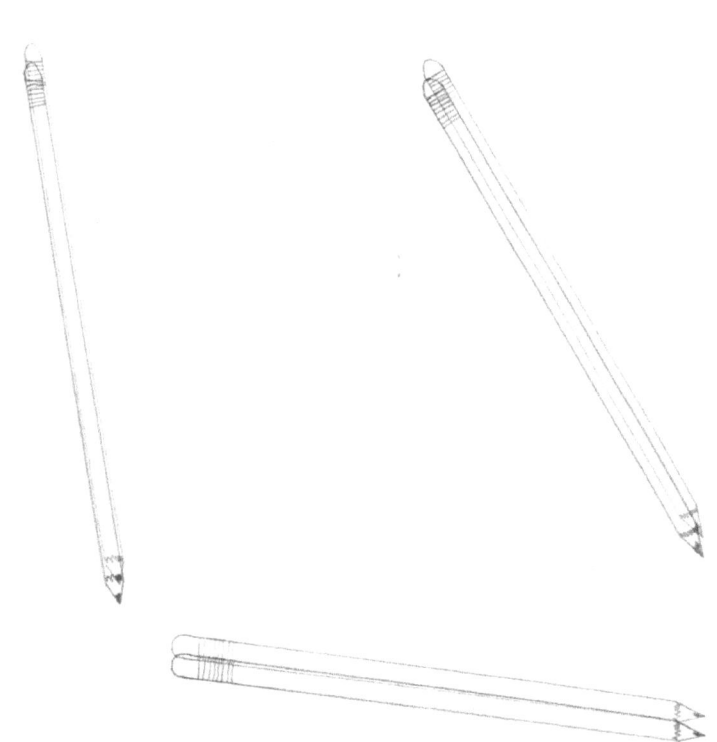

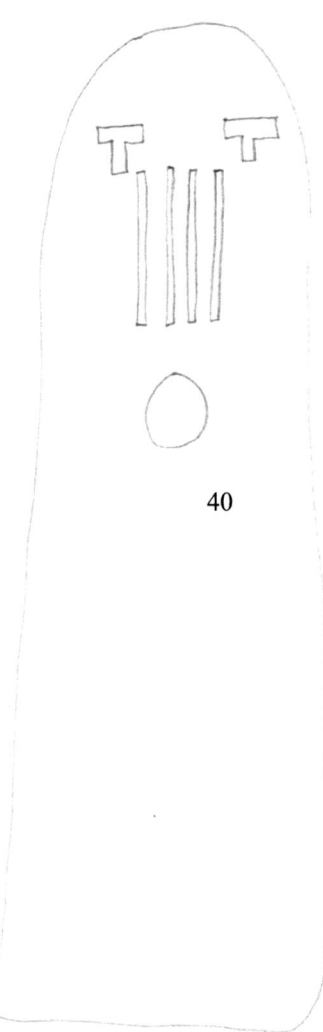

40

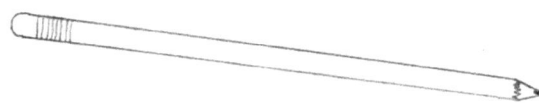

Grapes

41

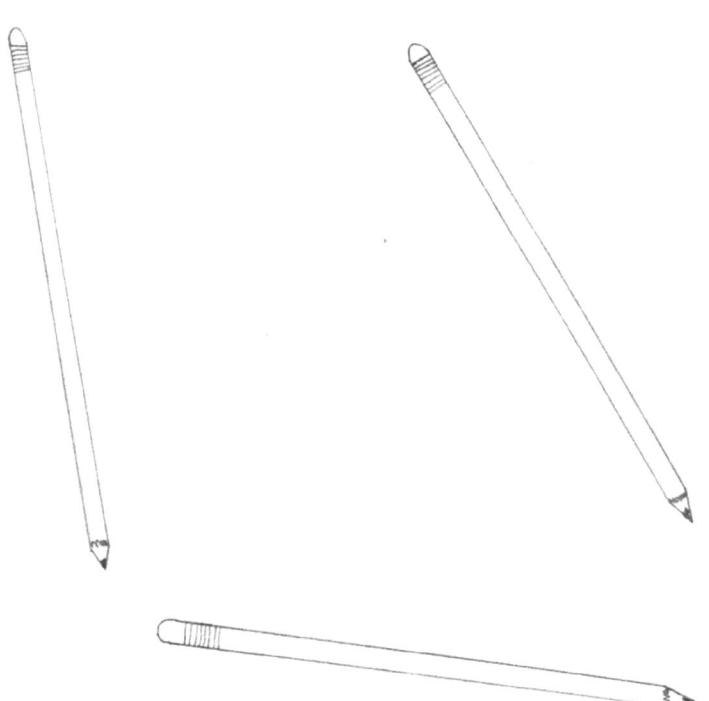

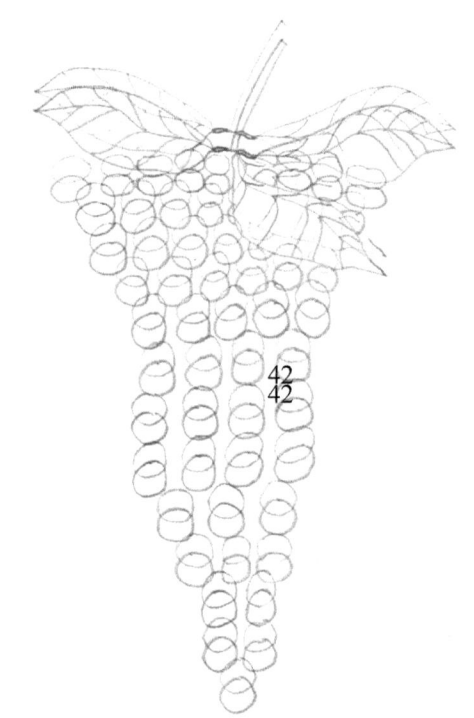

42
42

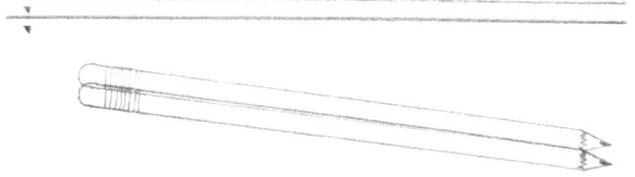

City
City

43
43

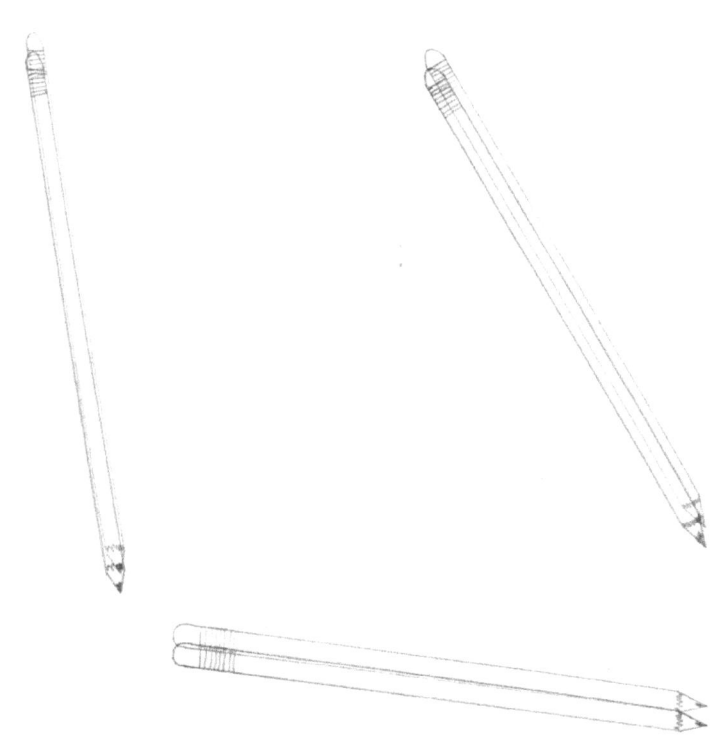

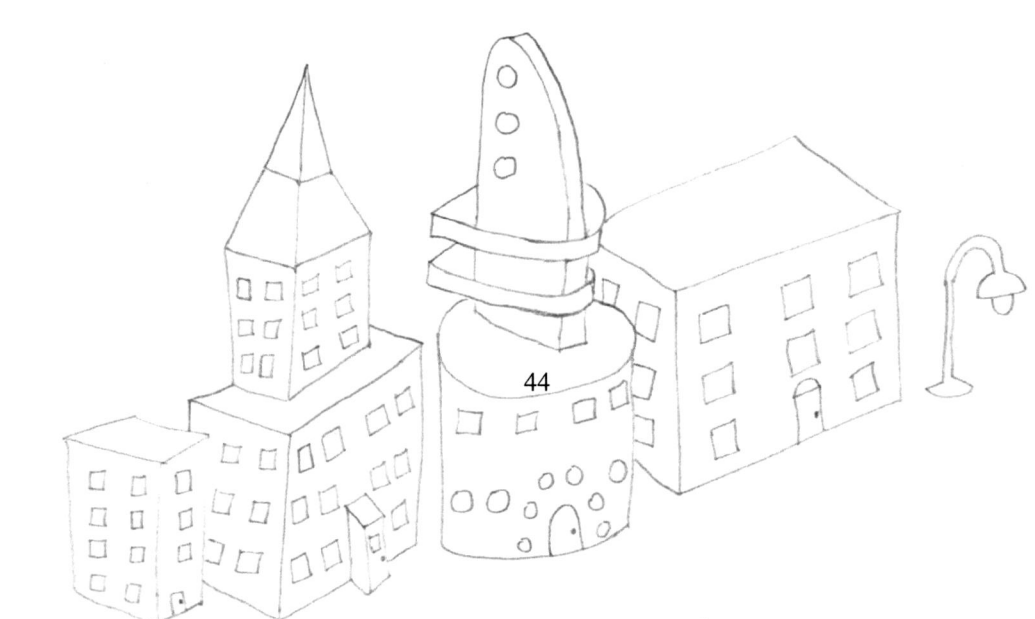

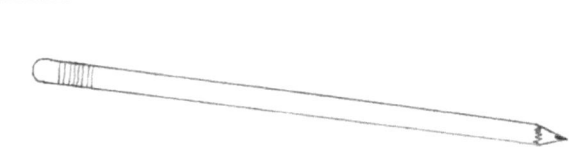

45

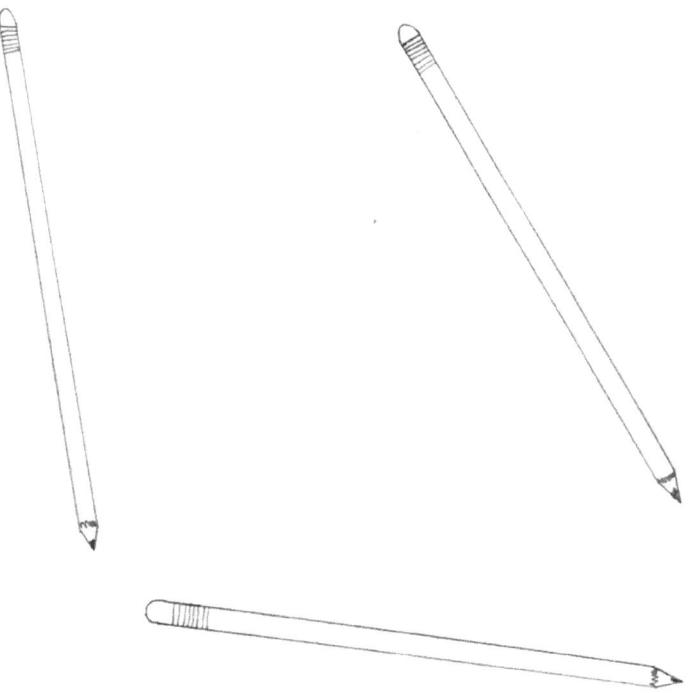

www.ingramcontent.com/pod-product-compliance
Lightning Source LLC
Chambersburg PA
CBHW051929210526
45473CB00006B/2187